Training the Driving Pony

ALLAN D. CONDER

ARCO PUBLISHING COMPANY INC.

219 Park Avenue South, New York, N.Y. 10003

All it takes to make a good pony
is a job for the pony to do,
and a pony that will do the job.

Published by Arco Publishing Company, Inc.
219 Park Avenue South, New York, N.Y. 10003

Copyright © 1977 by Allan D. Conder

Library of Congress Cataloging in Publication Data

Conder, Allan D
  Training the driving pony.

  1. Driving. 2. Ponies. 3. Horse-training.
I. Title

SF305.C66   636.1'6   76-770
ISBN 0-668-03942-8 (Cloth Edition)
ISBN 0-668-03951-5 (Paper Edition)

Printed in the United States of America

A question most often asked:

"How come you drive ponies instead of big horses, mister?"

"I drive ponies instead of horses for the same reason people drive compact cars. They will go as far and as fast as I want to go, and do it cheaper."

Contents

	INTRODUCTION	7
1.	GENTLING THE PONY	9
2.	HARNESS TRAINING	21
3.	GROUND DRIVING	35
4.	HITCHING (PUTTING TO)	55
5.	BACKING	65
6.	TEAM PONIES	69
7.	TRAINING THE SMALL RIDING PONY	81
	CONCLUSION	86
	INDEX	94

Illustration Credits

Don Goodall supplied the photographs on pages 24, and 79, 88. Neil Nichols supplied all other photographs in the book.

All of the pen and ink sketches were drawn by Donna.

Introduction

This will be a "how to" book—"how to" train a driving pony and "how to" teach a future driving pony the fundamentals that will prepare him for more serious and advanced training.

You cannot buy experience, you must earn it. The next best alternative is to borrow it. To that end and with that intent, I will lend you my experience. Use what will work for you and discard the rest.

No two people and no two ponies act or react alike. Keeping that in mind, I offer the method that works for me, and hopefully it will be of some help to you.

When you complete this training program, you will not have a finished product, but you will have a pony schooled in the basics of driving, ready for any type of advanced training.

This book is written for the person who has never trained a driving pony—a person with some experience with ponies who would like to try his hand at training one or two driving ponies, just for fun.

The pony may be a young pony you raised or bought, or he may be a trained riding pony you want to train for driving.

A pony running loose is by nature light, supple and collected. The weight of a rider automatically removes this lightness, suppleness, and collection until it is returned through training. A driving pony that has never been ridden and is pulling a very light load will retain a large amount of this lightness, suppleness, and some of his natural collection unless they are removed by poor driving and careless handling.

Do not forget everything you have learned while riding and handling riding horses or ponies, but set this knowledge aside until after you have read and understood this book.

There is no body contact between the driver and the pony as there is in riding. Your only contact with the pony while driving is through your hands on the lines, your voice, and the whip. A good driver uses the lines to tell the pony what to do, not by the strong-arm method of overpowering the pony, but by light wrist and finger pressure on the lines. He uses his voice to tell the pony when to do something, not in a loud voice for the onlookers, but in one- and two-word commands said quietly for the pony alone. The whip is the only other contact the driver has with the pony. It replaces the leg pressure of riding in order to collect and advance the pony, and is never used for abuse.

A fact overlooked by many people is that it is just as important for a pony in heavy harness and hitched to a heavy load to be light, supple, and collected as it is for a riding pony or a pony in fine harness hitched to a light vehicle.

When you train any type of livestock, patience is a virtue; knowledge, skill, and a willingness to learn are absolute necessities.

CHAPTER ONE

Gentling the Pony

I will take for granted that you have a pony at home and are ready to start training. First, be sure that the pony is large enough for the work you have planned, since a small pony can easily be overloaded. What size load do you have? Be sure you are not making plans which will overload and overwork your pony.

Do not use a stallion as the first pony you train to drive. If your pony is of a high enough quality to keep as a stallion, put him in the hands of a professional trainer. If he is not, geld him and train him yourself. My first choice is and always has been geldings, although I have trained and driven fillies with equal success. A gelding's behavior is about the same every day. When in season, some mares and fillies are very difficult to handle and drive. Under these circumstances, they take the pleasure out of pleasure driving.

A pony ready for training should be two and a half to

Newly purchased, barely halter broken, never groomed, under-fed, and hungry, but occasionally a poor looking prospect will make a good finished driving pony.

three years old. A four-year-old or older pony will be too big, tough, and hard to handle as a first pony for you, a novice, to train.

To start training a green, completely untrained pony, the first point of business is to catch the pony. There he stands: four furry legs, two big scared eyes, and a shaggy bundle of hair. "Catch the pony—How?"

It will be nearly impossible to catch the pony in an open field. Run the pony into a small pen, box stall, or other small well-fenced enclosure. Don't try to be a know-it-all hero with your first green pony. You won't impress the pony. In fact, the only one impressed may be your doctor, and he will only be impressed with how much damage a small wild pony can do to an adult. A green pony is not mean, just scared. He will protect himself and keep you from catching him in any way he can. The pony may kick, strike, bite, or run right over you. All he wants is to get away and you are in his path. You are sure to lose a wrestling match with the pony if you do catch him. However, there *is* a better way.

To catch and hold young ponies the first few times, I use a hurdle. This is the cheapest and easiest way I have found to catch and handle young ponies, and I find it to be entirely safe for both trainer and pony.

Here are the materials needed and instructions for building one hurdle:

one sheet of ⅜″ (1cm) plywood cut to 6′ (1.82m) length
two 2″ × 2″ × 4′ (5cm × 5cm × 1.2m) planks. An
    8′ × 2″ × 4″ (2.4m × 5cm × 10cm) will make two
    hurdles.
eight 3″ (7.6cm) carriage bolts

ten feet (3m) ⅜″ (1cm) rope

three eye bolts (with bolt ends or lag screw ends, as needed)

This hurdle was built for 48″ (12 hands) ponies; smaller ponies will need a lower hurdle. Try a hurdle 45″ × 6′ (1.14m × 1.82m) for ponies 45″ (11.1 hands) and under. The one shown has been used to train ponies from 46″ (11.2 hands) to 52″ (13 hands).

If you use the hurdle with the pony facing a wire fence when caught, use a piece of plywood to make a solid wall in front of the pony. A 2′ × 4′ (.61m × 1.2m) piece of plywood would be right for most ponies. Fasten the plywood solidly to the fence.

Build your hurdle to fit both you and your pony. It is better to have the hurdle too long than too short, too high than too low. If you train a larger pony later, and want the hurdle to be taller, add another 2″ × 2″ (5cm × 5cm) piece to each end, letting them protrude past the bottom edge far enough to raise the hurdle to the desired height. Be sure to place the carriage bolt heads on the plywood side, next to the pony. Always have the plywood side of the hurdle next to the pony. Use the rope, cut to proper length, to make hinges between the eye bolts in the wall and the ½″ (1.2cm) drilled holes in the hurdle. Knot a piece of rope in the middle hole on the rear edge of the hurdle, run the pony into the corner, swing the hurdle closed, and tie it to the eye bolt with the rope. Tie with a half bow knot for quick release. The hurdle should be pulled as snugly as possible without actually squeezing the pony.

You have caught your pony. If the wall he is facing is higher than his head, he can't get away. The pony will not

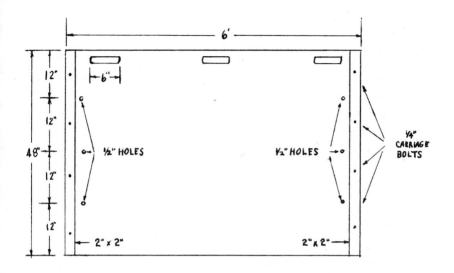

OUTLINE OF BOX STALL OR SMALL WELL FENCED PEN

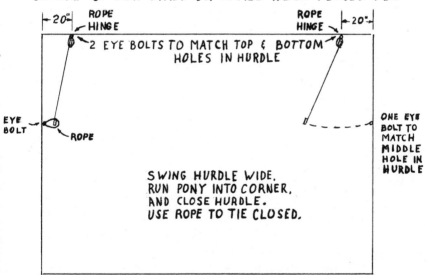

Diagram of hurdle and outline of box stall or small well-fenced pen.

be able to kick or strike at you, or to injure himself. Should he back up, the rope holding the hurdle closed will stop him. Caught in this arrangement, the pony will feel safer and fight less. He will, like most caged animals, think the hurdle is to protect him from you, not you from him.

More experienced trainers may look on this method of catching and holding a pony with displeasure. In training your first young pony, you will find this method practical and safe for both you and the pony. A hurdle built using the plans given will require little ability to build and is not expensive. Best of all, it *will* work.

What you do next and how you do it will have as much bearing on the final outcome of the pony as any single part of the entire training. Forget all the scenes you have ever seen showing a cowboy on one end of a rope and a wild-eyed outlaw horse on the other end. Cowboys are professional horsemen by occupation, while you are a novice.

Remove all distractions from the training area: children, dogs, other ponies, friends and relations. This is a time for you to concentrate on the pony and for the pony to concentrate on you.

Take a few minutes and talk to the pony. Don't make any move to touch him at first. Give him a few minutes to relax. All the pony has on his mind is keeping as much distance as possible between you and himself. Closed in behind the hurdle, the pony cannot kick or strike you and he cannot run, so the only thing left for him to do is bite. Do not give him a chance to bite; do not try to touch his face, ears, or head the first day.

The pony will begin to relax; when he does, start rubbing him with the flat of your hand. Make a fist and rub the pony

with your knuckles. Do not use the tips of your fingers: a
light touch from your fingers will feel too much like a fly
and will make the pony nervous. Rub firmly. Do not pat the
pony or he may take this as an attempt to punish him. Rub
the pony on his neck, withers, back, hips, and as far down
his sides as you can reach. This would be a poor time to
yell, wave your arms, or make any signs or sounds to scare
the pony. The pony may jump, rear, or otherwise try to
discourage you, but do not let it bother you, and go right on
with your rubbing.

Spend as much time as you can spare doing this (up to
one hour, morning and evening) for several days. The pony
will be much calmer in a day or two after he learns that you
have no intention of hurting him. Turn the pony loose after
each lesson.

The second day use a soft brush to brush the pony every
place you can reach, except his face and ears. On the third
day, use a flat nylon halter and put it on the pony.

Fasten a small rubber inner tube to the wall in front of
the pony, a little higher than his head. Tie the pony to the
inner tube with six inches of slack in the lead rope. Unfasten the rope holding the back of the hurdle. Keep the front
of the hurdle fastened and between you and the pony and
continue to brush the pony. The pony will pull back on the
lead rope as you start to brush him. This will be his first
halter lesson. The inner tube will pull just as long and just
as hard as the pony pulls. When he relaxes and steps forward, the pressure on the lead rope will be released.

The halter should fit snugly, leaving just enough room
for the pony to eat and drink. Turn the pony loose in the
box stall or small pen wearing the halter and dragging a

short (6′/2m) lead rope. Make sure there is nothing in the stall or pen on which the pony can catch the lead rope or halter.

Dragging the lead rope and being stopped short by stepping on the lead rope will soon teach the pony that the halter and lead rope are in control. Do not leave the halter on if you cannot check the pony every few hours or so. You can, after a day or two, walk up to the pony and step on the lead rope. As the pony starts to move away he will feel the jerk on the lead rope and will stop. You can then reach down and pick up the lead rope—and you have caught your pony.

I have never had a problem with this method of halter breaking, although I never turn a pony loose wearing a halter and dragging a lead rope any place other than his box stall or a very small training pen. I remove the halter every evening and replace it in the morning.

Up to now, you have been doing everything by reaching over the hurdle. The pony will become more calm and relaxed after a few days. Swing the hurdle open and place it against the wall out of your way. It would be best to leave the rope hinges tied for now; you may want to swing the hurdle closed in a hurry.

Don't rush at the pony—move slowly and easily and start brushing him as before. The pony may become upset and nervous without the hurdle, but *you* must stay calm. Continue to brush and talk to the pony. Take your time. You can, with patience, talk him out of any nervousness. When the pony will stand reasonably calm and quiet while being brushed, move the hurdle and inner tube to the opposite corner. A pony trained on one side must also be trained on his other side. Never train just one side of your pony; use the same lesson and method on both sides of the pony.

Lead the pony around the stall or training pen, You cannot out-pull a pony. Encourage the pony to step forward by using a light but steady pull-and-release motion on the lead rope. The pony will step forward to relieve the irritation and pressure as he did with the inner tube.

Do not use a "come along" while training a driving pony to lead. (A "come along" is a rope looped and placed over the pony's rump and around his quarters. As you pull the lead rope, you also pull the "come along," moving the pony forward.) Remember that the "come along" will fit the same place where you are going to be putting the breeching. Do not expect the pony to accept the breeching gracefully if you have used a "come along" on him.

Hang an inner tube on the wall over the pony's feed box; tie the pony and put in his grain ration. Brush the pony as he eats. Brush both sides, from neck to tail and from top to bottom, and don't forget to brush under his stomach, chest, and neck.

When the pony begins to accept being brushed all over, without requiring the hurdle, start picking up first one and then another of the pony's feet. Don't hold a foot for more than a few seconds, *then put it down*. Never let the pony jerk his foot away and put it down himself.

Each day, pick up *all four* of the pony's feet. Hold them a little longer each time, until you can hold each foot for a full minute. Clean out the pony's hooves, using a hoof pick. Your farrier will be your friend forever for your having given the pony this training.

Take hold of the pony's tail, and lift and hold it as you brush his quarters. This will be of great help later during harness training.

Use a soft cloth to wipe the pony's face. Rub his ears easily and softly; do not handle the pony's ears roughly. Rough handling of the ears can and probably will make the pony headshy—a very bad habit—making it difficult to halter and bridle him.

You will have spent several days or as much as two weeks gentling the pony to this point. Now you can lead the pony, pick up and clean his feet, brush and curry him all over, and most of all, you can trust the pony and the pony can trust you.

It is time to take your pony out of his stall and cross-tie him facing a blank wall. Leave six inches of slack in each lead rope, and curry and brush the pony on both sides in this new location for a day or two.

To begin blanket training, use a small throw rug, saddle blanket, or old bedsheet folded in half. Wad this up in your arms and walk up to the pony as you talk to him. Let the pony smell the cloth. Rub it along his neck, working your way back until you can carefully spread it over the pony. Spread it out as much as the pony will allow. Let the pony stand for a minute or two, then pull the blanket off—gently. Wad it up and repeat. Do this until the blanket can be spread completely over the pony. This could take several days. Put the blanket on from both sides, and pull it off from the side and over the rump. Don't flap or shake the blanket: be smooth and easy. Blanket training is very helpful on a driving pony. The more time you spend now, the easier it will be to train the pony to be harnessed. I prefer to tear an old chenille bedspread in half and use it for this job. It is large enough to cover the pony and is fairly heavy. The extra weight makes it lie smooth and teaches the pony that weight will not hurt him. Also, an old bedspread can be washed when it gets dirty. One bedspread should outlast several ponies, although one bedspread I used died an early death under my first pony, an old shod riding pony I was training to harness.

(Be very careful which old bedspread you use. I once tore a bedspread in half and found out it was not as old and used as I thought. This mistake cost me a great amount of conversation with my wife, and a new bedspread.)

This chapter is a rough outline of how to gentle a green, completely untrained pony—how to break the pony to halter, to lead and stand quietly while being brushed, let you pick up and handle his feet, and to know that the feel of something spread over him is not something to be feared.

This has been a two-way training lesson: first, it trains the pony; second, it will train you, the novice trainer, to have confidence in yourself and in your ability to handle a young, green pony. This alone makes it well worth the time and effort.

Other Uses for the Hurdle

You may want to build a small catch chute outside, near where you plan to wash and bathe your pony, before you take him to his first show or parade. Use two posts set deep, two feet (.61m) apart. Build another hurdle the same as the first. Use rope to tie the hurdles to the posts. You can tie the pony to the post, or nail a 2″ × 6″ (5 × 15cm) board to the outside of the post. If you tie the pony to the post, I suggest using plywood to cover over solidly between the posts. If you don't have a blank wall to use as instructed in this and later chapters, you can use this setup.

The first time you bathe the pony, turn the water hose on until it is only a small, gurgling stream of water. Keep as much hose as possible out of sight below the hurdle. Let the end of the hose stick over the hurdle and slowly move the hose end over the pony, letting the water soak the pony. The first time or two do not use soap when you bathe the pony. The pony may fight a bath at first. If you are only using water, you can stop anytime. If you are using soap, you must finish the bath in order to rinse the soap off. Always use lukewarm water; almost anyone would fight taking a bath in cold water on a breezy day, whether it be a pony or a person. Some ponies will take to bathing like ducks to water; others will need to be trained to bathing along with everything else.

Chapter Two will give you instruction on harness training. If you have followed the gentling lessons in this chapter, you should have no trouble with harnessing. If trouble develops during Chapter Two, review this chapter and use your hurdles to protect yourself while harnessing the first time or two. The hurdles will also come in handy should you need to doctor any of your ponies.

Harness Training

I must now assume the pony is broke (trained) to lead, and can be curried and brushed. Also, if the pony is old enough to work, he should at least tolerate a farrier.

Where and How to Tie the Pony

Tie the pony to a solid wall, one without openings. Use only one tie rope if possible. If the pony tends to be nervous or flighty, cross-tie him facing the wall. Do not tie the pony to a gate or fence with openings large enough for him to put a hoof or leg through.

Facing a blank wall seems to confuse the pony. Cross-tied and with no place to go, he will often stand quieter than when cross-tied in a driveway or to a hitching post.

Bridle

Use an open bridle (without blinders) with brow band and throat latch; an old riding bridle will do. Use a wire

A two year old filly, harnessed with the lines looped under the turn back strap, cross-tied to a solid wall, and ready for her first ground driving.

ring straight bar snaffle bit, a mullen mouthed snaffle bit, or a straight bar half spoon snaffle, which is also a good bit. Any time you have a choice, use the bit with the thickest bar. A riding pony should have the type of snaffle bit he is accustomed to wearing. Do not use reins.

Place your right arm over the pony's neck, close to his head, and holding the bridle in the right hand, put the bridle over the pony's face. Hold the bit in the palm of your left hand and raise it to the pony's lips. Insert your left thumb in the left corner of the pony's mouth, and press down gently on the bars (gums between front and back teeth) with your left thumb. This will cause the pony to open his mouth. Pull the bridle bit up into the mouth with your right hand. Be careful to get the bit over his tongue. Adjust the bridle to the pony, leaving the bit just a fraction lower in the mouth than normal.

Up to now, the procedure has been standard. Here is where I differ from most people:

Leave the halter on under the bridle or fit the halter on over the bridle, whichever works best for you. Tie your pony in his stall, wearing both halter and bridle, and give him one half the normal grain ration.

Continue to do this for several days, increasing the grain ration every other day or two, until the pony consumes his full grain ration in near normal time. A week to ten days should see your pony accepting the bridle bit readily, knowing he will soon be fed. Remove the bridle after all the grain has been consumed.

Contrary to what you may believe, I have not found this practice to make the pony's mouth sore. If at any time you feel the pony's mouth is becoming tender, cut back on the amount of grain given. However, I have never found this to

The proper way to put on a bridle.

be necessary. Use the bridle during only one feeding a day. You will not need this part of the bridle training on a trained riding pony.

Why an Open Bridle?

The use of an open bridle will make it possible for you to proceed with the harness training as you accustom the pony to the feel of the bit. The pony should know the sights as well as the feel and sounds of harnessing. A pony accustomed to wearing a blind bridle while being harnessed will need to be retrained to harnessing while tied with just a halter.

The Training Harness

Use a good stout set of single driving harness. The first mistake of many people training their first driving pony is to try to "save" their good harness. Please do not buy or borrow an old, worn, and possibly rotten set of harness with the intent of using it as training harness. This saving of pennies can easily lead to a loss of dollars, to say nothing of the possibility of lost skin and broken bones for both you and the pony.

If you do not have a heavy set of single driving harness, I suggest you purchase a set, new or used, being sure the harness is sound and as adjustable as possible. This will allow you to use it on a number of different size ponies. Keep this harness clean and oiled. Use it for training and as a spare set of exercise harness.

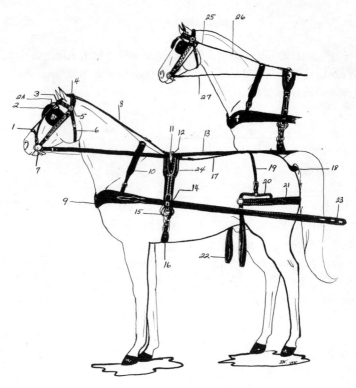

SINGLE DRIVING HARNESS

1. Nose band on overcheck
2. Blinders
2a. Blinder stay
3. Brow band
4. Crown piece
5. Bridle rosette
6. Throat latch
7. Half-spoon snaffle bit
8. Overcheck
9. Breast strap
10. Neck strap
11. Overcheck hook
12. Line terrent
13. Lines
14. Shaft tug
15. Shaft hold-down strap
16. Belly band
17. Turn back strap
18. Crupper
19. Hip strap
20. Breeching stay
21. Breeching
22. Hold back strap
23. Tug (showing adjustment)
24. Back pad
25. Gag runner loop
26. Side check
27. Lines

Lines

The lines (reins) that come with your harness may be too fine and short to use as training lines. I suggest you buy a pair of lines to use just for training. These should be ten to twelve feet (3 to 3.6m) long, and ¾″ or ⅞″ (12 or 12.3cm) wide. Buy the lines as wide as will feel comfortable in your hand. A set of single driving horse lines will do nicely.

The driving or hand ends (the ends away from the pony) should be brown English leather. Brown English leather will not stain your hands and clothes as black oiled leather will. Work any of the liquid glycerine soaps into the leather until it is soft and pliable. For convenience, I prefer snaps to buckles on the bit ends of the training lines.

The training lines should never have the driving ends buckled together. If there is a buckle on the driving end of the lines, cut it off. If the lines should be pulled through your hands in early training, the buckle could do a lot of damage to your hands.

Keep these lines clean and use them only for training. They will be a good investment, lasting for years and many ponies.

Shaft Tugs

The shaft tugs will need to be tied down to steady them during ground driving. Use the shaft straps to hold the shaft tugs steady, by buckling them into the shaft tugs. The shaft straps are a part of the bellyband and are normally used to hold the shaves down when the pony is hitched.

Backpad and Crupper

Remove the breeching from the harness when training a green pony. With an older riding pony, try leaving the breeching attached—only your own judgment can guide you on this.

Tie the pony as in bridling. Let the pony smell the harness. It may help if the harness has been used on a broke (trained) stablemate of the pony now being trained. A pony will usually relax and quickly lose his fear of and nervousness about strange things if you let him smell everything new before putting it on him. The pony will relax and lose interest quickly if it smells familiar.

As the pony smells the harness, slowly rub it against his neck. Take a few minutes to slowly work your way back until the back pad is resting in the proper place. This will be about the width of both hands behind the withers.

Let the crupper hang down on the left side of the pony. Reach under the pony and bring the bellyband up into position to buckle. Do not buckle the bellyband; pull it snug and hold it with your left hand. If there is an adverse reaction, you can hook a finger of your right hand in the rein terrent of the back pad. If need arises, you can release the bellyband and step away, taking the harness with you. The pony is unharnessed with nothing left to fight, while you and the harness are in the clear.

Start over from the beginning. Let the pony smell the harness and continue from there.

When the pony will stand quietly with the bellyband pulled snug and held by hand, buckle the bellyband. Leave room to place two fingers under the bellyband. Fasten down the shaft tugs.

Now for the crupper. Have the turnback (the strap fastening the crupper to the back pad) adjusted by guess. Gently raise the pony's tail. Do not let the pony clamp his tail down. The crupper should be unbuckled on the side near you (left side). Slip it under the tail. Be careful, and don't jab the pony with the buckle. It will help if the crupper has been unbuckled and spread into a wider "U" before you start to harness. Hold the tail with one hand and buckle the crupper with your free hand. Let the tail down gently.

Step back! The pony may jump, kick, or both. Give him room to react in any way he sees fit. Let the pony stand for a few minutes until he becomes familiar with the feel of the crupper. Adjust the turn back strap until the crupper is pulled just barely snug under the pony's tail.

Some few ponies never really accept a crupper. Most of the time this is due to a lack of patience and care in putting the crupper on the first time.

Leave the halter, bridle, back pad, and crupper on and tie the pony in his stall. Give him the grain ration. Remove the harness and bridle after all the feed has been consumed.

After several days, the pony should stand quietly while being bridled and having the back pad put on, the bellyband tightened, and the crupper put in position and buckled. Take your time; you will be surprised at how quickly the pony will learn.

I do not recommend the slip-on type of crupper, without buckles. This style of crupper takes too much time and effort to put on a nervous pony.

Put on this much harness for three or four days, or until the pony is completely at ease during harnessing, before adding anything new.

Breeching

With a pony that has been ridden, this part of the training may be combined with the preceding one.

Add the breeching to the harness. As you harness, lay the
breeching over the pony's back as you put on the back pad
and crupper. After all else is ready, lower the breeching to
the proper position, which is low on the pony's quarters.
The breeching should hang about even with the pony's
flank.

Leave the pony tied for a few minutes, allowing him to
get accustomed to the feel of the breeching. Be careful since
he may kick. Let him work it out. Talk him out of it if he
starts to fight the breeching, pet and rub him as you talk to
him. Quite often the feel of the breeching down low on the
quarters will upset the pony more than all the rest of the
harness.

If there are no problems, tie the pony in his stall to feed
as before. Stay nearby, since the pony may start kicking at
the breeching and become entangled in his harness.

Breast Collar

The next piece of harness to add is the breast collar. This
is the only piece of harness that can be old and somewhat
worn. Save the good breast collar that came with your harness for later use.

Put the breast collar on and run the traces through the
shaft tugs. Mark the traces a few inches past the shaft tugs,
and remove the breast collar. Cut off the ends of the traces
as marked, and rivet or sew a one-inch ring into the end of

each trace. Run the traces through the shaft tugs and buckle the hold-back straps from the breeching to the rings on the breast collar.

This modified breast collar will be good for no purpose other than training the pony to harness and ground driving.

Tie the pony in to feed fully harnessed, and again, stay close. If the pony starts to fight the harness, he could become entangled. The breast collar and breeching will make a continuous line of leather around the pony. It should fit snugly enough to stay in position, and loosely enough to allow the pony to walk and trot freely.

This serves two purposes: the pony will know the feel of the breast collar and there is less chance of his going cold shouldered (refusing to pull) when you begin to hitch. Also, the breeching will be held in place and will not bounce against the pony's quarters, possibly causing him to kick, when you start to ground drive.

A riding pony should only need one or two days between adding the breeching and adding the breast collar.

General Instructions

In each of the preceding steps, *do not hurry*. When a problem comes up, stop—and go back to the previous step. Start over from there, take your time, move easily, and try to figure out what caused the problem.

Blend each part of the training sequence in with the one preceding it. As the pony begins to accept each new part of the harness with reasonable calmness, add the next part. Do not let yourself or the pony become bored.

Talk to the pony as you work—let the pony know your

voice. What you say is not as important as the tone of your voice.

Do not abuse the pony at any time. Be patient. The pony is young and unsure about this new development in his life. Hurrying and rough handling will teach the pony to dread harnessing and he will react in the only way he knows: by fighting you and the harness every step of the way.

After you have gone through the entire harnessing lesson, continue to harness the pony for several days or until the pony accepts all of the harness without any fight. Don't expect too much. You may be well into the ground driving lessons before the pony is completely relaxed during harnessing.

A green pony should have each new piece of harness added after several days; a trained riding pony may only need one or two days before adding more harness.

A good time to start harness training is in late winter or early spring when the weather is unfavorable for other pony work.

When, in your judgment, the pony is becoming bored and is ready for a change, harness the pony completely. But this time change to the blind bridle that came with your harness. Do not fasten the overcheck.

Remember, a blind bridle is just that—blind. The pony cannot see in any direction but straight ahead. Speak to the pony before walking close to him or touching him. The pony will not be able to see you and may not hear you. If you walk up and touch him without letting him know you are there, the pony may kick, not with malicious intent, but in fright.

Time, weather, etc., may prevent you from advancing the pony to driving lessons when the harness training is completed. Should this happen, harness the pony every time you are going to be spending any length of time at the barn.

Tie the pony someplace other than his regular stall; the driveway of the barn is ideal. Go on with your work; this will let the pony become accustomed to the blind bridle and keep him accustomed to the harness. It will help him to learn that noise and commotion that he cannot see will not hurt him.

One advantage to the entire sequence of harness training lessons as outlined is that it will add only a few minutes to your chore time each day. However, if the method of harness training given above is too slow and prolonged for your use, try the following:

Use the same sequence of harness training lessons as described above. Be prepared to spend forty-five minutes to one hour once a day, or thirty minutes to forty-five minutes twice a day.

Put each part of the harness on and take it off several times. Finish each lesson by letting the pony have his grain ration while tied and harnessed. Add a new part of the harness each day.

A week's time will see the pony fairly well trained. With this short harness training method, you must go right on to ground driving without delay. This will let you combine the harnessing lessons with the ground driving lessons.

I dislike this quicker method. If for any reason you have a delay of a week or more between harness training and ground driving, the pony may forget the harness training, and to start over will consume more total time than the slower method.

You may ask "Why spend all this time on harnessing?"

Have you ever arrived at the makeup ground for a parade, after the parade has started, knowing you had to unload, harness, hitch, and fall in line before the parade passed you by? Did you ever have one youngster come out of the show ring with your one good set of harness and know you must help unharness and then harness another youngster's pony before the next class? Then, and only then, will you appreciate and understand the need for a pony trained to stand quietly while you throw the harness onto him.

It is not only nerve-racking but it is also embarrassing to have your peers stand around with their ponies all shined, polished, harnessed, and ready to go while there you are, with the entire family helping to harness an outlaw that doesn't want to be harnessed!

CHAPTER THREE

Ground Driving

Equipment Needed for Ground Driving

The method I use to start training a pony to drive is to ground drive in a ring or training pen. My barn lots were laid out with this in mind, so I have a permanent pen 36′ × 36′ (11m × 11m).

You can use any place with at least one square corner. If your barn has a driveway 8′ or more wide by 20′ or more long (2.4m × 6m), it should do. Otherwise, fence off a corner of your barn lot or pasture. You can buy four feed lot hog panels from any feed or hardware store that sells fencing. These panels are 16′ long and 32″ high (4.8m × .81m). You can use two to a side, wiring them inside a post, 18″ (.45m) from the ground. Use one steel post every 8′ (2.4m). If you do this in conjunction with an existing corner you will have a square ring 32′ × 32′ (9.7m × 9.7m) with a minimum of cost and effort. When not in use, this pen can be taken down and stored out of the way until it is needed again.

Whip

You will need a whip for training. Use one of the light whips with a fiberglass core, four and a half or five feet long (1.3 or 1.5m). Remove the lash that comes with the whip; replace it with a piece of very soft leather one inch by six inches long (2.5cm × 15.2cm). This type of lash will draw the pony's attention without really hurting him.

Shoes

Wear good shoes that are comfortable for walking. Be sure the soles will give you firm footing on the surface of your training ring. A bad slip at the wrong time can put you in the middle of a bad situation. I have a story about this which I will relate later.

The following instructions are given in detail, with several repetitions. It is better to be bored now and have the facts in your mind than to make a mistake the first time you drive the pony. A serious mistake the first time you drive can set a pattern that will be hard to break.

Starting the Pony

Bridle and harness the pony. Add the driving lines. Buckle or snap the lines into the bit and run them through the shaft tugs with the traces. Make two or three large loops in the lines and slide the looped lines under the back pad for the time being. *Do not fasten the overcheck!*

Lead the pony into the training ring. You will be leading

The proper position for the driver to hold the pony straight for the first ground driving.

a harnessed pony. Be careful; don't let the harness catch on a gate latch, door handle, etc. This can ruin your harness and make the pony gate shy—a very bad habit.

Place the pony near the fence, about half-way between the corners, with his right side near the fence.

This description of the pony's first driving will be given for a right-handed person. However, since two of my three daughters are left-handed, I have learned through working with them that it is best for a left-handed person to reverse the entire procedure.

You may have a helper to hold the pony. If not, tie the pony to a fence post and take down your lines. Stand behind the pony and to the left. Stay as close to the pony as possible but keep out of reach should the pony kick. The left line should come from the bit through the shaft tug to the left hand. The right line will come from the bit, through the right shaft tug, and around the pony's quarters above the hock to your right hand.

Make one or two large loops of the excess lines. Practice carrying these loops with the ring and little fingers of your left hand. Should the need arise, open your two fingers and the looped lines will fall free. Learn to use your thumb, first, and index fingers to hold the left line. *Never* carry the lines in such a way that they could become pulled tight around your fingers, hand, or wrist. *Never* take a half hitch in the lines for a better grip. It would be better to let the excess lines drag behind you than to let your hand become entangled in the lines. In the event of an accident you could be dragged and not be able to turn loose. This could lead to a bad injury for you.

It will be to your advantage to have your whip standing against the fence where you plan to tie the pony.

Now, holding the lines in the left hand, speak to the pony. Remember, he is wearing a blind bridle and cannot see you. Step up on the left side and unfasten the hitch lead. As you step back to the left and rear of the pony, pick up the whip in your right hand.

There is a very definite reason for each of the directions listed below:

A. *Do not fasten the overcheck.* A young pony in the confusion of first driving may find the overcheck too restraining. This may cause the pony to throw his head and/or rear to get away from the overcheck bit. The rule here is: use as few aids as possible. (In rare cases, the pony may back up to escape the overcheck bit—this can be dangerous to you.)

B. *Run the lines through the shaft tugs.* This low position of the lines will discourage the pony, should he want to rear. The lines will accustom the pony to something touching his back legs, which will put you ahead when you start using the traces in hitching. If the pony kicks, the bit will punish him then and there.

C. *Stand to the left and rear of the pony* (to the right and rear if you are left-handed). A right-handed person should stand far enough to the left so that his right hand is directly in line with the left shaft tug. The pony will want to turn around to the rear to find out what is behind him. In the position described, the fence will keep him from turning right, and the right line down low under his rump will give you the leverage to keep him from turning left.

D. *Carry the whip in your right hand.* It is customary to carry the whip in your right hand while driving, away from your passengers and away from the oncoming traffic. In training you want the whip in the hand with which you are most dexterous.

In driving, the whip is used for the same purpose that the legs and heels are used for in riding—to move the pony forward and to collect the pony. The whip is your one means of preventing the pony from backing up when all else fails.

The whip is an implement of use and should never be used as an instrument of abuse. Use the whip sparingly and lightly in most instances. Be careful; do not "whip sour" the pony by harsh and unnecessary use.

Never use the lines to hit the pony. You cannot use the lines to slap the pony without jerking the bit. This means you are telling the pony to "go" with the lines and telling him to "stop" with the bit, which is very confusing to the pony.

Here you are, to the left rear of the harnessed and bridled pony, the excess lines properly looped in your left hand, the whip and right line in your right hand. The pony is standing free except for the lines. What now? You have five seconds or so before the pony realizes he is, in his opinion, free.

Putting the Pony in Motion

Gently pull the left line an inch or two (2.5 to 5cm), or a little more than taking up the slack; release the right line slightly. As you pull the left line use whatever term you prefer to put a pony into motion. If he doesn't move (and most ponies won't) pull his head to the right a little, repeating the phrase.

This filly is properly harnessed for ground driving, although the breeching is just a little low.

Here I prefer the time-honored "get up," said slowly, distinctly, and firmly. Why? "Get up" is difficult for the pony to confuse with other commands that will be used later. Do not use other sounds, such as clucking your tongue, hissing through your teeth, etc.; this will only confuse the pony. Do not say "get up" unless the pony is standing still and you want him to move.

If the pony hasn't moved on the first two tries, add one more part to the starting lesson.

The third part of the starting lesson is to take the right line with a free finger of the left hand, and then reach up over the pony's back to the shoulders (withers) with the whip. Do not strike the pony on the back or hips; this will encourage him to kick. As you say "get up" the third time, pull the left line slightly and tap the pony lightly on the withers with your whip. Take the right line in your right hand quickly. If you continue to hold the right line as you use the whip, there is a chance that you will jerk the line and hurt the pony's mouth.

Let us go over the starting lesson one more time in its entirety. This is one lesson that must be firmly in your mind *before* you start the first driving lesson.

After releasing the hitch lead and taking your position to the left rear of the pony, turn the pony's head to the left a short distance with a gentle pull on the left line as you say "get up." Wait a moment. If there is no response, turn the pony's head to the right a short distance with a gentle pull on the right line as you say "get up." Wait a moment. If there is no response take the right line with a free finger of the left hand, reach up and over the pony's back with your whip; as you say "get up" for the third time, turn the pony's head to the left a little and tap the pony on the withers with the whip. Take the right line in the right hand quickly.

If the pony doesn't move, let him think it over for a couple of minutes and then go through the starting lesson again. Be more firm with your hand and voice and use the whip more sharply.

If possible, coax the pony into moving without using the whip. The pony that is a gentle pet will be the most difficult to start. Firmness, without abuse, is essential.

Be prepared. The pony should move now—it may be just a few steps, or there may be an explosion.

When the pony starts to move, go with him *at a walk!* If the pony stops, use the starting lesson again. Discontinue the starting lesson any time the pony starts to move whether it is after the first pull of the line and the first "get up" or after using the whip.

Some ponies will try to break into a run. DO NOT LET THE PONY OUT OF A WALK! To control the pony's speed, move with him *at a walk*. Brace yourself. Hold your hands steady, let the pony walk into the bit, and don't jerk the lines. Put equal pressure on each line, holding the pony straight as he moves. Do not let yourself become confused. I repeat, DO NOT JERK THE LINES.

The pony may be scared, confused, and possibly angry after you have first used the whip. You have told him "go." Remember, you have not as yet made any effort to teach him at what speed to "go." Do not jerk the lines and punish the pony for too much speed. I repeat, hold your hands steady.

It will only be a few steps to the corner. Your position to the left rear with equal pressure on both lines should keep the pony from turning away from the fence. Let the corner stop him.

Let the pony stand in the corner for a minute or two, say "get up," and turn his head to the left out of the corner. Keep the slack out of the right line or the pony may turn around and face you.

If the pony doesn't start to move as you turn his head out of the corner, use the starting lesson. As the pony starts to move, swing in behind to the left rear and move with him.

Continue to drive in this manner for several turns around the ring, letting each corner stop the pony. Stop and start at each corner until the pony begins to show signs of understanding the starting lesson, then stop at every other corner. When you approach a corner you intend to pass without stopping, use your left line two or three steps before you reach the corner. Relax your right line as you turn, but do not let it go slack as the pony may turn around and face you. I suggest you do not drive longer than twenty or thirty minutes the first day.

The next day do the same thing in the opposite direction. Place the pony with the fence on his left side. As you stand to the right rear of the pony, the left line will pass through the left shaft tug and around the pony's quarters; the right line will pass through the right shaft tug to the right hand.

Use the same starting lesson as before; turn to the right as you drive. Stop at each corner and, as before, when the pony shows an understanding of "get up" and a slight pull on the line to start, you can then stop at every other corner. Drive for twenty or thirty minutes.

The next day drive one way around the ring for twenty minutes, then reverse your direction by turning into the fence. As the pony turns, change the lines in your hands to hold the pony close to the fence. Use the same term each time to start the pony. Do not vary. Do not try to stop the pony by voice and lines at this time; walk him into a corner to stop.

In confusion, a pony may take one or two steps backward at times. Don't punish him for this; he will get over it on his own.

An older, trained riding pony will sometimes back up from contrariness. In fact, they may try to back right over you if you let them. Any time this happens, use your whip quickly and sharply on the pony's lower back legs. Never do this with a young green pony—only with an older riding pony that should know better.

Balking

Once in a while you may encounter a pony that will be sullen and not move. A pony that knows you want him to move but refuses is said to balk. A pony that doesn't know what you want or expect of him from lack of experience and therefore stands still in confusion and refuses to move, can be said to be sullen. Most horsemen will refer to this as "sull."

Don't continue to whip a pony that sulls. After you have been through the starting lesson two or three times without response, use your whip lash to tickle and irritate the pony. Do this, not by striking the pony, but by dragging the whip lash over the pony's withers, through and over his mane as far forward as the bridle, without touching his ears, saying "get up" from time to time. This irritation is too far forward for the pony to kick at, and it will do little good for him to rear as the irritation is above him. The pony can't escape by lowering his head. The only way for him to escape this irritating "thing" is to step ahead. Stop using the whip as the pony starts to move.

Drive in both directions around the ring; as the pony shows signs of understanding, drive across the ring away from the fence. Make figure eights using the entire ring; turn back along the fence. This will teach the pony to answer the bit at the same time he is learning "get up."

Day by day, begin to move further out toward the end of the lines. This will let you walk a much smaller circle than the pony and will be very helpful if you have two or more ponies in training at the same time, saving many steps.

As training continues, walk behind as well as out to each side as you drive. Be more firm with the starting lessons.

The pony will soon reach the point where a gentle pull on one line and a quietly spoken "get up" will start him in motion without hesitation. Then—and only then—will you and the pony be ready for "whoa."

To reach this point in the training may take only a few days or as much as ten days to two weeks. No two ponies are alike. Sometimes the most stubborn and contrary pony to train becomes the best pony at the end of the training period. Don't overlook the fact that some ponies are just plain dumb, even if you did raise them from your favorite mare.

Teaching "Whoa"

Do not expect the pony to stop in one stride. Drive as before. Pick any two places on opposite sides of the ring other than a corner. As you approach the place you have chosen to stop, use your fingers to give a very light pull (equally on both lines) as you say "whoa," then hold your hands steady. Slow down your walk to a stop and let the pony stop by walking into the bit. Do not haul back on the lines. Don't expect the pony to stand still. All your efforts have been concentrated on "go." It would be asking too much to expect the pony to learn "whoa" in one lesson.

Stop twice each time around the ring, stopping at the same places each time.

When the pony stops, expect him to be very restless and try to move ahead and/or to back up a step or two. Do not punish him for this restlessness. To punish the pony now will only confuse him. After stopping the pony, hold your hands steady; each time he moves ahead and hits the bit say "whoa." Do NOT JERK THE LINES. Let the pony stand for a few seconds and then start him forward again. Teaching the pony to stop will take several days; teaching the pony to stand dead still in his tracks, without moving, will take longer.

Say "whoa" and at the same time give a gentle pull (equally on both lines) to indicate to the pony that you want to stop. A firm but gentle pull on both lines should stop the pony. After a few days, the pony should stop within two strides and it will no longer be necessary to stop walking and brace yourself to stop the pony.

You are now blending together the two lessons "get up" and "whoa." As soon as the pony begins to show understanding, drive away from the fence across the ring. Do figure eights and start and stop any place and every place. As time passes, let the pony stand still for a longer time until he is standing for two or three minutes at each stop. Finish the day by standing still in the middle of the ring for five minutes or more.

You and the pony will become very bored with the ring. *Don't become impatient. This is the greatest mistake a trainer of any type of livestock can make.*

Now that the pony will start, stop, and stand, you are ready for a new lesson.

General Information

A pony that has been treated too harshly with the whip or that has been hurried too much during the teaching of "get up," will give you a great deal of trouble in learning "whoa" and to stand quietly.

Take your time. Repeat the lesson over and over until the pony shows definite signs of understanding. Be sparing with your whip. Use your fingers and wrist; be gentle but firm with your hands.

At times the pony may want to run. When this happens, brace yourself, clamp your arms to your sides, and fold your wrists in toward your belt buckle. Let your wrists take the shock of the pony hitting the bit. Your wrists are much stronger and tougher than a green pony's mouth.

I prefer to leave the overcheck loose until much later in the training. You may, for one reason or another, feel the overcheck is needed. If so, leave four inches (10cm) of slack. Every other day take up one hole in the adjustment until there is only two inches (5cm) of slack. Leave it there for now.

During training, the purpose of the overcheck is not to raise the pony's head, but to keep him from carrying his head lower than normal.

Rearing

With the lines in a low position running through the shaft tugs, there is little chance of the pony trying to rear. If the pony continuously tries to rear, *look first to yourself!*

Why is the pony trying to rear? Are you too rough handed and hurting the pony's mouth? Are you driving for too long at a time so that both you and the pony become tired and impatient? Are you giving the pony ample advance indication that you want to stop? Is the overcheck too tight? If so, loosen it to four inches (10cm) of slack and leave it there for a few days.

Give the pony every chance before you correct him for rearing. Be sure he is not scared, confused, or hurting before you correct him.

If the pony continues to rear without reason, use your whip under the pony's stomach. Use your whip *only* while the pony has *both front feet* off the ground.

Open Mouth

During the early driving lessons, the pony may get into the habit of holding his mouth open. This is a bad habit and hard to break if it continues for too long. The bad habits *of the driver* that cause a pony to rear are the same ones (in a milder form) that cause a pony to work with his mouth open.

After a few days, the pony may relax and respond to the bit without opening his mouth. Give the pony a chance and check out all possible causes. If the habit continues, use an elastic band around the pony's nose, above the bit. Make up a band of ¾" (2cm) elastic with a heavy coat hook and eye fastener. This should be long enough to go around the pony's nose above the bit. Leave room to slip one or two fingers under the band without pinching. The purpose of this is not actually to hold the pony's mouth closed, but to put pressure and strain on the jaw muscles when his mouth is open.

Sight and Sound

Did you ever drive or ride in a show ring with pennants flying all around the rail and overhead for decoration? As you finish the last few days in the ring, it is a good idea to tie white and colored rags to the training ring fence. As the pony progresses, fasten two or three soft drink cans to a string or light rope, tuck the end of the rope down inside your belt and drag it behind you as you walk. Don't tie the rope you may want loose in a hurry! Have a radio playing, shuffle your feet as you walk, and let your children and the family dog hang on the fence as you drive. Drag the whip stock down the fence (the side without the children, of course).

Rein Terrents

Change your lines from the shaft tugs to the rein terrents on the back pad. Do this any time the pony steps out and walks straight away without the use of force to hold him in a straight line.

Running Martingale

You may or may not want to add a running martingale. A running martingale will help put a more attractive head set on the pony. During the early training a pony may learn to depend on the martingale and you will lose some of your control when you take it off. I prefer to wait until a later time.

It is very difficult to use a running martingale on a team pony; therefore, a pony trained with a running martingale will give you problems when put into a team.

Now you have a pony that will start, stop, and stand quietly, one that is not afraid of strange sights and sounds, a pony with confidence in you and in which you have confidence.

Open the gate; drive in the open, through the yard, near the road, letting the pony see and hear the traffic. Let the children ride their bicycles along with you—better now than at your first outing away from home to show off your new pony. If you wish to show the pony in trail classes, you can drive the pony through your practice course. Do not (for the present) try to back the pony; he is not ready for it as yet. Chapter Five is on teaching the pony to back.

No matter how hard you try not to, you will overlook something in your outside driving that will scare your pony the first time you leave home. For example, I have one pony that is absolutely certain a pony-killing monster lives in every rural mailbox we pass.

Jointed Snaffle Bit

After you have driven the pony outside the ring for a few

This pony just knows that there is something terrible in every mailbox we pass.

days, you may need firmer control than the straight bar snaffle bit has to offer. I use a wire ring jointed mouth snaffle, with flat bars. The joint should be tight. This bit will put more bearing surface on the pony's mouth and is easier on the pony's mouth than a bit with round bars. If the bit has half spoons, so much the better.

If the pony starts chewing at the bit, tossing his head or showing other signs of discontent after changing bits, wait a few days; if this continues, change back to the straight bar bit for a few days.

Always look a new bit over carefully. Be sure there are no burrs or casting marks which may bruise or cut the pony's mouth. Any of these you find should be filed off and buffed smooth.

The most important rule in bitting is quite simple: ROUGH HANDS REQUIRE A MILD BIT.

One evening, a friend and his family drove into our farm pulling a horse trailer. He asked if we had time to help with their pony. We told him to unload the pony and tell us his troubles.

The pony was an old pony, forty-six inches tall and about 400 pounds. This old pony was as good a child's pleasure driving pony as I knew of, and I couldn't guess what the trouble could be.

Well, it seems that the son of the family (all of seven years old and seventy pounds) had been riding the pony without success. The father laid out one of the wickedest displays of jawbreaker bits I have ever seen. He told me that no matter what bit he put on the pony when his son rode, the boy couldn't control the pony. The pony would walk and run flat out at full speed—nothing in between.

I put a snaffle bit like the bit in the pony's driving bridle in the riding bridle, and held a heart-to-heart discussion with the father and son on the proper use of hands. End of trouble.

Whether riding or driving, when in doubt, try a milder bit.

A pony that is a well-trained riding pony should go through the entire sequence of training lessons as outlined, from harnessing through driving, in two to four weeks.

A young green pony should complete the same training in four to six weeks.

Remember, the most contrary, stubborn, hard-headed pony will often be the best trained one in the end. A sleepy, easy-going pony will often wander through the entire training without giving you one minute of trouble. This is the one to watch out for. If and when he wakes up, it will almost certainly be at a time and place that is to your disadvantage and embarrassment.

There is one final item to be added to this chapter. What is your pony's name, and does your pony know his name? It will be to your advantage to precede "get up" with the pony's name. The first few days of driving may be too confusing for you to bother, but as you become more sure of yourself, start using the pony's name.

Say "Frank, get up"—or whatever your pony is named. This will teach your pony to respond to his name. There are several advantages to this: a team pony can be moved up into the collar without disturbing his teammate, and a pony can be started without bothering the other ponies when you are driving in a group. Your tone of voice when speaking the pony's name will make him aware of whether you are pleased or displeased with him.

CHAPTER FOUR

Hitching (Putting To)

The preceding chapters have only one purpose: to prepare you and the pony for this chapter.

You have a pony and harness. I suggest you buy, and use for training, one of the light metal pony-sized carts that are on the market. These light two-wheeled carts, which are equipped with rubber tired bicycle-type wheels, are not expensive and will last for years. A light two-wheeled cart will follow the pony's every move and is much better for training than a four-wheeled vehicle.

Harness and bridle your pony. This time use the regular breast collar that came with your harness. Lay the traces over the pony's back; they will stay better if you put them under the turn back strap. If you have a helper to hold the pony, so much the better; if not, cross-tie the pony as before.

Bring the cart to the pony; do not take the pony to the cart. Pull the cart behind the tied pony several times to let

Put to a cart and ground driving in the open for the first time.

the pony see and hear the cart. The pony will learn to know the sound of the cart and to know that this sound holds no danger for him. It is important to accustom the pony to the sound of the cart. Remember, this noise will follow him with every move he makes after he is hitched.

Line the cart up with the pony and lift the shafts higher than the pony's back. Do not try to pull the cart forward while holding the shafts level with the shaft tugs. There is too great a chance of jabbing the pony with the tip of the shafts. Speak to the pony—remember that he cannot see you—and pull the cart forward until the front ends of the shafts are even with the shaft tugs. Carefully lower the shafts and run them through the shaft tugs. Pull the cart forward; do not bump the pony's hindquarters with the single tree and cross bar (the brace between the shafts).

Take down the traces, and slip each trace over the end of the single tree. There should be a leather thong near the outer end of the single tree; run the end of the thong through the small hole in the extreme outer end of the single tree. This will keep the trace from accidentally slipping off the single tree. This is referred to as "the keeper."

Carefully, but firmly, pull back on the cart until the traces are pulled tight. The tip of the shafts should be even with the point of the pony's shoulder, leaving a foot or more of room between the cross bar and the pony's hindquarters. If the cart is too far forward or backward, change the traces. There should be two or three holes in the outer end of each trace for adjustment.

Next, wrap the shaft straps one or more turns around the shaft on each side and buckle. Leave enough slack in the buckled shaft straps to allow you to raise the cart shafts an inch or so. When using a four-wheeled vehicle, the shaft straps must be pulled just snug; this will keep the shafts from bouncing.

Stop, step back, and take a look. The shafts of a cart should be level or at a very slight incline to give the cart proper balance. The shafts can be raised or lowered as needed by raising or lowering the shaft tugs equally on each side of the pony.

There will be a loop of metal or leather under each shaft just in back of the shaft tug. This is where you wrap and buckle the hold-back strap. Be careful that each strap is tightened evenly, otherwise the breeching will hang and pull unevenly. With the pony standing square and even, and the cart pulled back until the traces are tight, each buckled hold-back strap should have two inches of slack.

The breeching, in its position around the hindquarters of the pony, acts as the brake. As the pony slows or stops, the breeching draws tight around the hindquarters of the pony, and by being attached to the shafts, slows or stops the cart. The pony can move the cart backward by backing into the breeching.

Is the pony completely and properly harnessed and hitched to the cart? Ask yourself this question each and every time you hitch the pony, then look to be sure. Make it a point to look at every strap and buckle.

You will need a larger fenced ring to drive the hitched pony. A ring 30′ and 60′ (9.1m × 18.2m) is as small a ring as you can use. A larger ring would be much better.

Open the doors and gates wide. Lead the pony into the ring. Be careful as you swing the pony away from the wall where he was tied so that you do not catch the tip of the shaft on the wall. Take a firm hold of the pony to lead him;

watch carefully that you do not catch the cart on the door or gate.

Stop the pony in the center of the ring. When the pony is completely calm, take down your lines and move back until you are standing behind the cart. The lines and whip should be held in the same way as when ground driving without the cart. Do *not* attempt to get in the cart for this first driving of the hitched pony.

Take a firm hold on your lines and put the pony into motion. Drive in a large circle, but do not drive close to the fence. It is possible to hook the tip of the shaft in the fence. There will be a difference from ground driving, for you will be asking the pony to turn into the shaft. Until now the pony has been free to turn in his own way. At first, most ponies will resist pushing against the shaft to turn the cart.

Do not use a long solid pull on the line to turn the pony. The pony can set his mouth against the bit and continue to walk straight ahead. Pull and release the line with short, light, quick movements of your fingers and wrist. The pony cannot brace himself against this kind of action on the bit, and will slowly begin to turn. Learning to use your fingers and wrist to give this series of quick light pulls and releases of the line will be a major step in training yourself to be a knowledgeable driver of a driving pony.

Heavy handed, rough handling of the pony when he first resists turning into the shaft will destroy much of his lightness, suppleness, and collection. This loss will require you to spend long hours retraining the pony to his natural way of going. Be light and gentle but firm with your hand.

A very few ponies may continue to resist turning the cart by pushing against the shaft. Most often, these will be well-trained riding ponies that have been taught to move away from leg pressure in making a turn. You are asking the pony to do the opposite of what he has been taught to do—to turn into instead of away from pressure.

If all else fails, use your whip to help turn the pony. At this time, the whip should be used to tap the pony on the neck and shoulder. Do not punish the riding pony for refusing to turn by harsh and impatient use of the whip; he is only doing what he has been taught to do as a riding pony.

You may need to step up alongside the cart in order to reach the pony's shoulders with your whip. If you are turning left, walk on the right side and tap the pony's right shoulder.

This, too, is a secret of good driving: Use your lines to tell the pony what you want him to do, use your voice to tell him when to do it, and use your whip to encourage him to do it right and on time.

Walk and drive behind the cart for a few days, or until the pony will answer the bit without hesitation. Drive in circles, make figure eights, and start and stop the pony everyplace and anyplace.

Once every few rounds of the ring, stop the pony and let him stand for a minute or so. You may well ask, "Why worry about teaching the pony to stand? I want to go, not stand." Standing is boring and you want to go; the problem is that so does the pony. I cannot emphasize strongly enough the importance of teaching the pony to stand quietly while hitched.

For those of you planning to use your pony for pleasure driving, remember that the pony must stand while you and your passengers enter and leave the cart. Some of you will continue to train your pony in the advanced and refined manner of a show pony. A show pony will be required to "Come in and line up facing your ringmaster." A show pony that will not stand is not only maddening but also very embarrassing.

By the second or third day of driving hitched to the cart, the pony should be driving as well as he did during the ground driving lesson. Stop the pony in the center of the ring, take up the slack in your lines, and quietly and smoothly step into the cart. *Sit down immediately!* Never stand in a cart.

Do not attempt to start the pony for a few minutes. Let the pony become accustomed to your weight on the shafts. Should the pony become restless and attempt to move, encourage him to do so; otherwise, you will need to put him in motion.

Drive as before. Go both ways in the ring, do figure eights, small and large circles, start, stop, and stand, until the pony will work as well with your weight in the cart as he did in the ground driving ring.

You will find little need for the whip now. I suggest you place it in the whip socket and drive by line and voice alone. In the event of an emergency, the whip will always be close at hand when carried in the whip socket.

Only you can decide when the pony is under complete control and answers all commands given by bit and voice. Then it will be time to encourage the pony into a slow jog trot. As the pony walks out, take up the slack in your lines and coax him into a trot by using your voice. *Do not* use the whip. "Click" your tongue, or make some sound that is easy for you in order to urge the pony into a trot. Do not make

Step into the cart, sit down, and drive. Note that the back pad is set too far ahead in this picture.

First time on the road and moving at a trot. The whip is laid close to hand in case it is needed.

the same sound in asking the pony to trot as the sound you use to put him in motion from a standstill. This will be the pony's command to trot from now on.

From this point on, practice each and every day that you can spare the time. You and your pony will get better and better with each practice.

You have now completed the full course in training a single driving pony. Your pony will start, stop, and stand. Most important of all, he will pull the cart with you, his trainer, as passenger.

CHAPTER FIVE

Backing

Teaching the Pony to Back

I have purposely not mentioned backing the pony until now. Teaching the pony to back can be the most difficult lesson of all if it is not handled with patience, persistence, and gentleness.

A pony you raised from a foal should have been halter broke, taught to lead, and to stand tied while still with the mare. This is also the ideal time to start teaching the pony to back. Each time you lead the foal, take a short hold on the lead rope while standing in front and slightly to one side of the foal. Say "back," pull and release the lead rope, lifting his chin as you do so, until the foal takes a step or two backward. You can use your other hand against the foal's chest to encourage him to step back. Do this every time you lead the pony. By the time the pony is well trained to lead, he will be backing at a light pull on the lead rope and the voice command "back." If you do this each time you halter and lead the pony, he should back on voice command alone when he is a yearling.

Backing is an unnatural movement for the pony and must be taught. A pony running loose in the pasture will almost always rear and spin or simply turn around to reverse direction. You will seldom see a pony back of his own free will and on his own accord. A pony must raise his head and lower his rump to back properly. A completely untrained pony you have bought to train as a driving pony can be taught to back as you train him to the halter and to lead. Use the same method as that given to train a foal to back. It will take more time and patience to teach an older pony to back than it will take with a foal. Do not become discouraged, and continue to back the pony each time you halter and lead him.

The pony will be well on his way to backing on the voice command "back" and a slight pull on the lead rope by the time you have finished the bridle and harness training.

When the pony is completely harnessed and bridled, stand in front of and slightly to the side of the pony, take hold of *both* lines six inches from the bit, and say "back" while giving a slight pull equally on both lines. Work on this each time you start to ground drive and before you unharness the pony each day. Do not at first try to back the pony while ground driving. Only after the pony understands "get up" and "whoa" and is driving and standing well, should you back the pony while standing behind him.

A pony taught to back in this manner will back on the voice command "back" and little more than taking the slack out of the lines.

A pony trained to back during the ground driving lesson

will give you no problems backing when hitched. It will be easier on the pony, when hitched, to learn to back an empty cart. I would suggest you adjust the breaching a little higher than normal on the pony's quarters when first teaching him to back the cart. This will give him a chance to place his quarters lower in the breaching and use his weight more efficiently to back the cart.

Placing the instructions on how to train a pony to back in a separate chapter may be somewhat confusing to you. Teaching a pony to back is in itself very confusing to some people. However, with a separate chapter, you can study and concentrate on the instructions on backing a pony without interruption.

This pair of fillies is showing impatience at being made to stand.

CHAPTER SIX

Team Ponies

I strongly urge that all team ponies be put through the driving lessons for a single driving pony *before* being put into a team. A future team pony that has finished this much training is ready to be put into double harness with his prospective teammate.

The training ring you have been using will be rather small for a team. I would suggest using a large fenced lot for ground driving the team, if one is available. Learning ground driving as a team should take two or three days. Afterward, a few days driving in the open would be a good investment in time.

One of the oldest, most practical, and accepted methods of training a new team pony is to harness and ground drive him with an old, wise team pony. A wise old pony that handles this job well with any and all new green ponies is referred to as a "hitch" pony. There is no proper description of a hitch pony, for each is an individual suited to the job and his owner. It is not unusual to enter a barn full of young draft horses and see one older horse that just doesn't seem to fit in with the rest of the horses. When asked about this, the owner will often say "that's my hitch horse." To a knowing horseman, no further explanation is needed.

When they are first harnessed together, leave the halter on under the new pony's bridle, and tie the lead rope back to the "hitch" pony's hame ring, leaving a bit of slack in the lead rope. A couple of days of ground driving should see the new pony ready to be hitched (put to) to a wagon with the "hitch" pony as a teammate.

I have occasionally found myself with two green team ponies and no hitch pony. If you are in this situation, use the same method. Tie each lead rope to the other pony's hame ring, leaving more slack in each lead rope when hitching a team of green ponies. Ground drive these two ponies harnessed together for several days. A much longer time will be required than when using a "hitch" pony.

As soon as you and both ponies react as a three-member team in starting, stopping, and standing still, then you will be ready for the next lesson: hitching (putting to).

Team Harness

It would seem appropriate to give some hints on harnessing a team. First and foremost, fit the collars. I suggest you find a harness maker to fit the collars for you. For those fortunate enough to live in a rural community, I suggest you ask around until you find someone who has worked horses on the farm and ask for his help. For those of you who must do it yourself, turn to page 76. Read and study the illustrations and information.

HOW TO FIT A COLLAR

Build two squares as pictured, making sure the corners are reinforced to hold them square. Use 1" × 2" (5cm × 10cm), making the short side 12" (30.4cm) and the long side 18" (45.6cm).

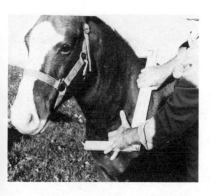

Put the two squares together to make a "C." Place it on the pony's neck ahead of the withers. Put two fingers inside the "C" and against the pony's neck at the bottom.

Hold the squares tightly, remove, and measure as shown. This is the length of the collar needed. For a heavy-necked pony, go to the next inch larger. For a thin-necked pony, use the next inch smaller.

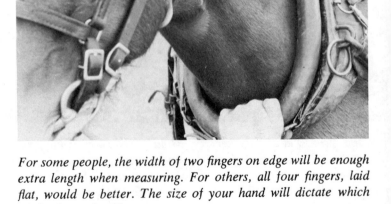

For some people, the width of two fingers on edge will be enough extra length when measuring. For others, all four fingers, laid flat, would be better. The size of your hand will dictate which method you should use.

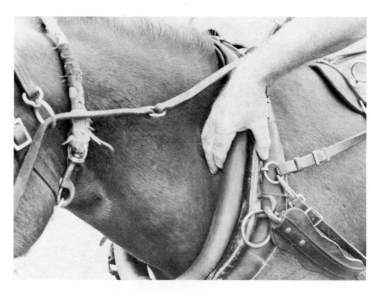

The width of this collar is right, but it is too long.

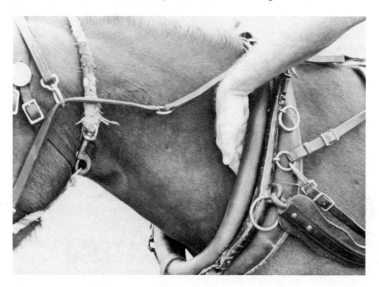

This collar is both too long and too wide. More horses and ponies have had their shoulders and necks ruined by collars that are too large than by collars that are too small.

A collar that is too short and narrow. This will seldom injure a pony simply because he cannot or will not be able to pull without choking.

Three years of hard use has proven this to be a well-fitting pony collar.

From left to right: a regular draft collar; a half sweeney draft collar; a kay collar, with hames, tugs, and choke strap, used in formal driving; and a regular collar for driving harness.

DOUBLE DRIVING HARNESS

1. Nose band on overcheck
2. Blinders
2a. Blinder stay
3. Brow band
4. Crown piece
5. Bridle rosette
6. Throat latch
7. Snaffle bit
8. Overcheck
9. Overcheck hook
10. Team lines
11. Turn back strap
12. Crupper
13. Pole strap
14. Choke strap
15. Tug and buckle adjustment
16. Belly band
17. Back pad
18. Traces (showing adjustments)
19. Liverpool bit
20. Gag runner loop
21. Side check
22. Hame and top hame strap
23. Choke strap
24. Bottom hame strap

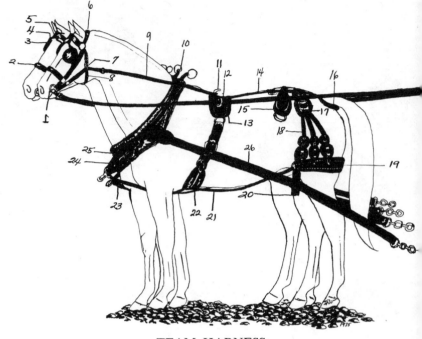

TEAM HARNESS

1. Snaffle bit
2. Nose band
3. Blinders
4. Blinder stay
5. Brow band
6. Crown piece
7. Gag runner loop
8. Throat latch
9. Side check
10. Hames and top hame strap
11. Side check on overcheck hook
12. Line terrents
13. Back pad
14. Turn back strap
15. Hip drop
16. Crupper
17. Trace carrier
18. Hip strap
19. Breeching
20. Lazy straps
21. Hold back strap
22. Belly band
23. Pole strap
24. Breast strap and snap
25. Bottom hame strap
26. Trace
27. Heel chains

The next most important item is the bridle. Fit them carefully and mark them so you will not make a mistake and put them on the wrong ponies.

For a proper fit of the bridle, put the bridle on the pony and center the blinder (the leather shield over the eye) over the center of the eye. Adjust the crown piece first and then adjust the bit. The bit should pull up slightly in the corners of the mouth. Be very sure the bit is of the proper width. A bridle with a separate overcheck bit should have this bit removed. The overcheck can be buckled into the driving bit for training purposes.

The rest of the harness should fit pretty much like a set of single harness. Take care in harnessing the first few times if you are using heavy harness (such as draft horse harness) since the heel chains (chains at the end of the traces) will rattle and could spook the pony.

The lines will be different from those of your single pony harness. The lines have a check rein (the short buckled-on rein) that goes to the inside ring of the teammate's bit. The long continuous line (direct line) goes directly from your hand to the outside ring of the bit.

When the team is standing square and even, the direct line should go from your hand through the rein terrent to the outside bit ring. The check rein is buckled onto the direct line and passed through the other rein terrent and will cross over to the opposite pony's inside bit ring with about two inches (5 cm) of sag. This means that if the lines are taken off and spread out, the direct line will be approximately six inches (15 cm) shorter then the check rein.

You will need a wagon or buggy when driving a team of ponies. It must be equipped with a tongue or pole rather than shafts. There will be a neck yoke and a double tree.

Ground drive your ponies for a few minutes with the lead ropes tied. For this first driving, it would be best to put the neck yoke on before starting to ground drive. Slip the pole strap over the end of the neck yoke. Next, run the breast strap through the ring in the outer end of the neck yoke and snap in the opposite hame ring. Do this with both ponies. The neck yoke must hang evenly; if it does not, adjust the breast strap on the harness. When using team driving harness with a buggy, the neck yoke and harness will be different. There will not be a breast strap on the harness. There is a strap buckled around the neck yoke. Run this strap under the collar and buckle it back into itself, after having first put on the pole strap.

Have your wagon or buggy out in the open; drive your team to the wagon, and swing one pony over the tongue. Back the team until they are standing even with the outer end of the tongue.

At this point it is advisable to have a helper to hold the ponies while you finish hitching. If the helper is not available, have the end of the tongue near a building or fence. The early training of being tied to a wall should hold the ponies still while you continue to hitch. For your safety, do not place the end of the tongue any closer than six feet away from the building. This will give you room to get out of the way should the team move.

Lift the tongue and run it through the ring in the center of and below the neck yoke. Wire the neck yoke ring to the stop on the outer end of the tongue. See the picture on page 79.

Never put yourself in a position, while hitching, in which you cannot reach the lines to stop the team should the need arise.

Team (pair) in heavy harness at the trot.

Going down a sharp grade, working against the breeching.

Take down an outside trace and hook it to the single tree, then take down and hook the inside trace. Step to the other side of the team and hook up the traces of the other pony. Lead the ponies ahead a step. The traces should be just snug and the neck yoke and breast straps should hang almost straight down with a slight forward slant from the collar to the neck yoke ring.

A team tied in too tight (traces too short) will have too much weight put on their necks and will not stand well. A team tied in too loose (traces too long) will cause the neck yoke to come off unless it is wired on. If the neck yoke comes off the tongue, you have lost all control of the wagon. A runaway, upset, or both is sure to happen. Be sure you wire the neck yoke on while training.

You are ready to step into the wagon or buggy. Sit down! Now, get out of the wagon. Look at each strap, buckle, trace, and line. Is your team properly hitched? Do not get into the wagon without one last check; you should know better by now. You should have no trouble, so drive as before. From now on, all you will need is time, patience, and practice.

Drive your team as though it were a single pony. You drive the outside (away from the teammate) not the inside (near the teammate) of your team. Watch, and drive both ponies at all times. Don't be guilty of "driving one and leading one."

The hitched team, standing straight and even with the direct lines just snug and the check reins with a small amount of sag where they cross, should have their heads straight ahead. If their heads are turned in or out, unbuckle and move the check rein until the ponies' heads are straight. Rebuckle the check rein.

CHAPTER SEVEN

Training the Small Riding Pony

Did you ever want to train a riding pony that was too small for your adult weight? Try using the same training lessons as in driving, using a saddle instead of a harness. When training a riding pony, you do not change to a blind bridle, but use an open riding bridle throughout the lessons. Tie the stirrups down and run the lines through the stirrups.

When the pony reaches the degree of training where he will start, stop, and stand, put a child in the saddle. Continue to ground drive the pony—this puts you in control so you can train the rider as well as the pony. Gradually let the rider take over control, using the riding reins, as you continue to walk behind, holding the driving lines for safety. This plan has worked well for me.

A few years ago, due to a previous loading chute accident, we had one pony that was afraid of all loading chutes. After the Illinois State Fair, Junior Department Horse and

Pony Show, this pony refused to load in the truck for the trip home. It was late at night and a number of other people were waiting to use the loading chute to load their horses and ponies. In addition to these people, a crowd gathered to watch the fun as we tried to load a balky pony—how embarrassing!

This pony stands 12:1–½ hh and weighs 600 lbs, so it was impossible to drag him up the chute. As a last resort, I put the riding bridle back on over the halter, and my daughter mounted the pony bareback and rode several circles at the foot of the loading chute. As they approached the loading chute I stepped in behind the pony and said "get up" in my nastiest voice. The pony had not forgotten the many hours of ground driving and what could happen to a pony that doesn't respond to "get up." He walked up the loading chute without one moment's hesitation. We received a nice hand from the crowd and a lot of unasked-for advice on what to do with a pony like that. We didn't use any of the advice.

I do not recommend this method of loading ponies, but it did work for us once when we really needed it. This pony had finished his lessons in ground driving eighteen months before the loading chute incident at the State Fair grounds. This story illustrates how well the early training stays with the pony.

I might add that this blue roan pony has taught three girls to ride and money cannot buy him from me (although he still doesn't care for loading chutes).

The Right Pony

Regardless of the future use planned for the pony, I use

these basic training lessons on every pony I have started to train for driving or riding.

Some people who train ponies will lead you to believe that they have never had a failure. I am not that fortunate. There have been ponies that were just wrong, from start to finish, for the work I had planned for them.

Pearly

Pearly was a filly I knew couldn't miss as a fine harness pony. She had flashy color, style, refinement, and excellent conformation, and if she had enough speed she might have made a roadster pony. This was not to be.

Pearly turned out to have the quietest, sweetest, gentlest temperament of any pony I have ever known. Most pony people would have called her plain lazy.

After I had put her through the lessons in driving, I sold her to a family with two little girls. These young ladies learned to ride and drive, using Pearly. They continued to drive her for several years after they outgrew her for riding. I understand that this filly has had four foals and has proved her worth as a brood mare. She has been sold and is now teaching her second family of children the fun and enjoyment of riding and driving a pony. Pearly proved me completely wrong when I picked her for a fine harness prospect as a two year old filly, and she proved me wrong again by turning into an outstanding child's pony.

Joe

At the other extreme, there was Joe! The gentleman who

sold Joe to me called him a started gelding. I have always wondered what he had started Joe on, rocket fuel, maybe? When I bought Joe, I was looking for a pony to match a mare I owned. My intention was to make a team out of Joe and the mare to use in parades and to give wagon rides to children. Both jobs require a rather quiet, steady pony.

After having Joe around for a few days, I decided to start from the beginning—from haltering, to currying and brushing, to bridle and harness training. I drove Joe in the training ring until I was worn out, but Joe was getting stronger each day, without, as it happened, learning much of anything. Finally, Joe had more or less progressed well enough so that I was ground driving him outside the training ring.

If I remember correctly, this incident happened early on Memorial Day morning, and I was killing time, pony driving, while my family was getting dressed and preparing a lunch to take on a picnic. With a wife and three daughters, this can be a long wait.

I started to drive Joe through a field of green oats. The oats were tall enough to tickle Joe's stomach. Joe jumped, my new leather-soled shoes slipped on the oats, still wet from dew, and down I went, still holding onto the lines, spread out and flat on my stomach! After I was dragged several feet by the lines, my weight pulled Joe to a stop. Slowly and painfully, I regained my feet and drove Joe back to the barn. My family came out of the house, expecting me to be ready and waiting to take them on the picnic, just as Joe and I went by on our way to the barn. I was driving with one hand and trying to remove the evidence of my trip through the oats with the other.

Some day, my family may forget Joe, but they will never forget, nor let me forget, the morning the oats were growing out of my nose, ears, shirt pockets, and belt buckle.. Nor will they let me forget how long they waited, this one time, for Dad to shower and change clothes.

For the rest of the day, my daughters kept telling our family and friends, "A very funny thing happened to Dad this morning, while he was driving Joe! Tell 'um the story Daddy, tell 'um the story."

Joe had "go" and no "whoa" when I bought him. Joe still has "go" and no "whoa." Today Joe is a moderately successful racing pony, under the guidance of a new owner, thank goodness.

After you have chosen a young pony to train and find, much to your sorrow, that the pony is not suited for this particular use, STOP. There is someone else who can use this pony. Don't let pride and sentiment force you into keeping a pony that is completely wrong for the job at hand. Admit to yourself that you made a mistake in choice of ponies. Sell this one, and buy or raise one better suited to your needs.

Most of us keep ponies for fun and pleasure. Why keep a pony that is not a pleasure to own and drive?

Trivia

Each show should have one driving class for newly trained driving ponies by novice trainers. This class should have two divisions, shown simultaneously:

A—The walk, trot, and runaway division: Winner to receive a blue ribbon, spotted with tears of fear and desperation.

B—The walk, trot, and balk division: Winner to receive a blue ribbon with the tail of the ribbon in shreds, symbolic of the gnashing of teeth in frustration.

All parade chairmen should have one multicolored ribbon to award to each driver-trainer who is driving a newly trained single pony or team of ponies in a first parade, for both driver and ponies: Each to receive a ribbon with the multicolors denoting blood, sweat, tears, bandages, aspirin, and black and blue bruises.

Remember, the name of the game is *fun and pleasure*.

Conclusion

This book has been written using simple terms and common words and descriptions to make it easier for the novice to read and understand. For example, rather than using the horseman's terms "near side" and "off side," I have used the everyday "left" and "right." Each chapter was written to stand alone, making it unnecessary to refer back to the preceding chapter for the job at hand.

During the harness and ground driving lesson, I cautioned you to leave the overcheck unfastened. Later on, there are instructions on how to accustom the pony to the overcheck. My preference is to fasten the overcheck after starting to hitch the pony, and then to leave it loose until putting the pony into more advanced training during the next season.

A ring to use during the ground driving lesson was described, as was a larger ring to use for driving the hitched pony. Before spending money building a ring, do take time to study your present facilities. Won't they do? Look

Hundreds of children and adults have taken their first wagon ride behind this team of ponies.

around you: with only a little change, you may have a pen, barn lots, driveways, etc., that will do without further expense.

The use of the whip by a novice may raise a question in the mind of more experienced horsemen. A novice will stay a novice until time and experience take him out of the novice class. You cannot become experienced by avoiding an issue. Therefore, in my opinion, it is better to give proper instructions on the use of the whip right from the start of the training lessons; much better than letting the novice receive poor instructions or no instructions at all.

Here is a list of aids and tools of the trade *to be avoided* by the novice at all cost: chain leads, running W, half running W, hobbles, Scotch hobbles, twitch, war bridle, and severe bits of all types. I do not object to nor criticize the use of these tools in the hands of an experienced trainer, but I strongly urge the novice to wait until some time in the future before adding them to his training methods.

Draft horses on the farm have been replaced by the tractor, dray horses of the city and village have been replaced by the truck, the family driving horse has been replaced by the automobile, station wagon, and pick-up truck. As the horse was being replaced by the motor, drivers and trainers of all types of horses were being replaced by the motorized chauffeur and the mechanic. The horse and pony industry came through this change from horse to motor as a hobby, where the riding horse and pony rule supreme.

Today there are more outstanding riders than ever before, and along with these riders, you will find many outstanding riding instructors and trainers of riding horses and ponies.

The problem is that there are few driving instructors and trainers of *driving* horses and ponies. Those you will be able to find are busy and expensive, and very few will have time to train a driving pony to be used as a family pleasure pony.

Unfortunately, what you will find plenty of are drug-store cowboys, fast-money artists, and the know-it-alls found in every business and hobby. The first two types will offer training and instruction for a price, and the last will offer free advice—all of it bad. Beware! Beware of putting yourself, your children, or your pony into the hands and at the mercy of one of these so called "horsemen." Before taking the help or advice of anyone, have him show you his trained driving horses and ponies. Go and watch him train a pony to drive, ask his price, and look over his facilities for training. A week or two of looking here and watching there will be time well spent.

Anyone with a love of ponies, a desire to learn, some extra time, and this book, can train a driving pony and in so doing, teach himself to be a driver and trainer of driving ponies.

These instructions are given in fine detail and it will take time to carry them out. Each new pony you train will take less time and be easier for you. If you continue to train driving ponies, in just a short time you will work out a formula of training lessons suited to you and your needs. You will, after training several ponies, find that the lessons on gentling the pony in Chapter One can be combined with the harness training in Chapter Two. Both will become one smooth lesson that will blend into the ground driving lesson of Chapter Three. Ground driving will be one continuous lesson, rather than several separate step-by-step lessons.

A pair of green fillies, showing a lot of promise.

On the completion of the training lessons given in this book, and the training of your first driving pony, your patience has been proved; you will have become skillful and knowledgeable, and your willingness to learn will no longer be in question. You are now the trainer of a driving pony. Novice is a word of your past.

GOOD LUCK!

The author's pride and joy: Sam and Charlie, a pair of grade geldings in heavy harness, put to a rack (hay wagon).

Index

Age of driving ponies, 9–11
Aids, 39
    to be avoided by novice
      trainer, 89

Backing, 45
Backpad, 28
Bad habits. *See* Habits, bad
Balking, 45–46
Bathing a pony, 20
Bellyband, 28
Bits, 23
  adjusting, 77
  chewing at, 53
  jointed snaffle, 51–54
Blanket training, 18–19
Blind bridle, 21, 25, 32, 33, 77
Breaking pony to halter, 19
Breast collar, 30–31, 55
Breeching, 30, 31, 58
Bridle, 21–25
  open, 21, 25, 81
  proper fit of, 77
Brushing a pony, 15
Buggy
  for team ponies, 77
  stepping into, 80

Cart
  hitching pony to, 55–58

stepping into, 61–64
type to use, 55
Catch chute, 19
Catching a pony, 11–12
Check rein, 77
Collars, how to fit, 70–74
"Come along" (rope), 17
Commands (voice), 54, 60
  "back," 65–66
  "get up," 42, 46
  to trot, 61–64
  "whoa," 46–48
Cross-tying pony, 18
Crupper, 29

Direct line, 77
Double driving harness, 75
Draft collar, 74
Driving
  ground. *See* Ground driving
  hitched pony, 59–64
Driving lines, 36, 38, 39. *See
  also* Lines (reins)

Feeding a pony
  with breeching on, 30
  with bridle on, 23–25
  fully harnessed, 31
Feet, picking up pony's, 17
Fillies, 9

Gate shy, 38
Geldings, 9
Gentling, 14–18
"Get up," 42, 46
Green ponies, 11, 19
  harness training of, 32
  time required for training lessons, 54
  training for team, 69–70
Ground driving, 35–54
  equipment needed for, 35–36
  for left-handed people, 38, 39
  for right-handed people, 38, 39
  starting lesson, 36–43

Habits, bad
  gate shy, 38
  headshy, 18
  open mouth, 49–50
Half sweeney draft collar, 74
Halter, 23
Halter breaking, 15–16
Harness
  heavy, 77
  single driving, 25–26, 55
  for a team, 70–77, 78
Harness training, 21–34
  general instructions for, 31–32
  patience and, 34
  short method of, 33
  slower method, 21–31
Headshy, 18
Hitching, 55–58
"Hitch" pony, 69–70
Hold-back straps, 58
Hooves, cleaning, 17
Hurdle, 11–14
  building, 11–12
  uses for, 19–20

"Joe," 83–85
Jointed snaffle bit, 51–53

Kay collar, 74
"Keeper, the," 57

Leading the pony, 17
Lead rope, 16
Lines (reins), 27, 50, 60
  for team ponies, 77
  See also Driving lines
Load, size of, 9
Loading chute, 81–82

Mouth
  open, 49–50
  sore, 23

Name, pony's response to own, 54
Neck yoke, 77, 78, 80

Overcheck, 32, 36, 39, 48, 49, 77, 87

"Pearly," 83
Pen, training, 35
Pole strap, 78
Ponies
  age of, 9–11
  gentling, 14–18
  green, 11, 19
  the "right," 82–85
  show, 61
  size of, 9
  team, 69–80
  training small riding, 81–86
Putting to. *See* Hitching

Rearing, 49
Reins, 27
Rein terrents, 50
Riding pony, training, 81–86
Ring, training, 87–89
  for driving hitched pony, 58
  for ground driving, 35
  for team ponies, 69

Rubbing a pony, 14–15
Running, 48
Running martingale, 51

Saddle, 81
Shafts, 57–58
Shaft straps, 57–58
Shaft tugs, 27, 38, 39
Sights, getting pony accustomed
    to, 50, 57
Single driving harness, 25–26
Size of ponies, 9
Smell, pony's sense of, 28
Snaffle bits, 23
    jointed, 51–54
Sounds, getting pony accustomed
    to, 50, 57
Speed, control of, 43, 48
Stallion, 9
Standing, importance of teach-
    ing, 60–61
Starting lesson for ground driv-
    ing, 36–43
Stirrups, 81
Stopping, 43–45
    on command of "whoa," 46–
    47
    in corner, 43–45
"Sull," 45

Talking to the pony, 31–32
Team harness, 70–77
Team ponies, 69–80
    driving, 80
    harnessing, 70–77
    hitching, 78–80
    running martingales and, 51
    training new, 69–70
Tongue (on wagon or buggy),
    77, 78, 80
Traces, 30–31, 57, 80
Trainers of driving ponies, lack
    of, 90
Tree, double (on wagon), 77
Trot, slow jog, 61–64
Turning hitched pony, 59–60
Tying the pony, 21

Voice. *See* Commands (voice)

Wagon
    stepping into, 80
    for team ponies, 77
Walk, 43
Whip, 36, 38, 39–40, 42, 43, 45,
    48, 49, 60, 89
"Whip sour," 40
"Whoa," 46–48

Yoke, neck, 77, 78, 80